YVR

YVR

by

W. H. New

OOLICHAN BOOKS
FERNIE, BRITISH COLUMBIA, CANADA
2011

Library and Archives Canada Cataloguing in Publication

New, W. H. (William Herbert), 1938-
    YVR / William New.

Poems.
ISBN 978-0-88982-280-1

    I. Title.

PS8577.E776Y87 2011   C811'.54   C2011-905935-5

We gratefully acknowledge the financial support of the Canada Council for
the Arts, the British Columbia Arts Council through the BC Ministry of
Tourism, Culture, and the Arts, and the Government of Canada through
the Canada Book Fund, for our publishing activities.

Published by
Oolichan Books
P.O. Box 2278
Fernie, British Columbia
Canada V0B 1M0

www.oolichan.com

Cover design by Gerilee McBride.
Cover image *End of Season*, 1993, lithograph by Jack Shadbolt, copyright
Simon Fraser University. Image of print 137/150 provided by Maynards.

Printed in Canada

for Peggy, Kathryn, Violet

stories, inventions,
histories, songs

CONTENTS

1. NOISES OFF

2.   REHEARSAL

3.   IN CONCERT

1. NOISES OFF

China Creek, Still Creek, Oppenheimer, Lam,
Choklit, Trafalgar, Ebisu, Elm—

Nelson, Kensington, Charleson, Grays,
Robson, Templeton, Thornton, Falaise—

Brewers, New Brighton, Bobolink, Glen,
McSpadden, Macdonald, McCleery, McLean—

John Hendry, Douglas, Prince Edward, Jones,
Matthews, Rosemary Brown, Maple Grove—

Lines

Often I have said *goodbye,*

      pulled down the blinds,
          locked the doors,
  left the city to wallow in its rivalries and said
          not me not me, embracing
       London Paris Hong Kong San Francisco,
         someone else's anywhere,
          and called it life,

    or thrown myself down mountainsides, called
      foxgloves and grizzlies my friends,
         told Rome be damned
          and left.

But here I am.

    Singing.

        That tug of danger, *home.*

We're born with gills, we say to strangers,
    laughing the pared shore, the daylong overcast,

   walking brash the quaking land, the theatre
     of seagrass:
             trolling wood, fire, anarchy
      and desperation,
        over the sediment,
        under the rain,

                              impulsive,
                  insecure.

        Sedges grow in the sidewalk cracks.
              The air is salt.
                  The river runs rough,
                          erosion—

Links

November: an overnight fog drifts in:

voices carry where the eyes don't reach

and turnip-coloured signs loom double-talk,
PHONE TO MORROW FOR YOUR COAL TODAY—

We hae meat says a butcher's window:
Inglis Reid on Granville advertising
sausages and haggis, *that ye can eat*—

Who's out there? People: here   and no

longer here: laughing their lives in quiet:

shouting passion, poetry, anger, blue
huzzah: weeping despair, bemoaning
failure, tripping through *avoir, savoir,*
trying out their tangled tongue—

My father, when he was happy, chanting
the Zulu praise song he learned years back
as a deckhand at sea—

My mother, when I didn't remember
to say please: *Who was your servant last year*—

Myself on stage at seventeen, singing
words I took exception to, *And in the West
There is a Nest*—

The foghorn off Point Atkinson sounds its
two-note against shipwreck, confusion—

So many others get lost in history, silenced by it,

stories they told, or might have, with them:

Ironworkers when the bridge collapsed in
'58:   you could see the Narrows
from up the hill on Dundas Street—where I
used to visit Lucy's, when I was nine and
walked her golden spaniel—

didn't know steel girders soon would
break like bones on the weight of the sea—

Kids on the street in '45, playing
hopscotch on V-E Day, chanting *The War
is Over*, not knowing what it meant: that
rationing would carry on, like Tojo
fear and the stick of a thousand slurs:
V-J Day still to come, the bomb and slow
revision—those stories—

Even tales of the terracotta nurses, who
perched for years on the side of the Medical-
Dental, then lapsed from myth like Florence
Nightingale, after the demolition—locals
called them the Rhea sisters (no Titans on
their mind, just *Dia, Pyo, Gono*)—they surfaced
again at the University, where new myths
fluttered every day, clutching the walls of
Technology Enterprise Facility
Number Three—

Words tumble off curbs, stagger into darkness,
twist cantilevered through the wet-cold air—

On a sidewalk outside Holy Rosary
a man tracks back and forth, mumbles
answers to the voices in his head, *Do it
now bugger devil bugger bugger cut it
down*—

In King George High the ESL class is
exercising HAVE: *He is having the
nightmares. She was had to tea party.
Are you having heat. Please, what is
difference, have and to hold?*

Wind-runners

take the sea wall in Stanley Park: it
beckons the sea, surprises walkers,
bikers, runners, lap and spray—

you think you're managing, you have the
right shoes, right gear—silk, fleece—
you could be Ace, Harry, Percy, Landy—

wind's in your face as you round past
Siwash Rock—suddenly you're skipping
fences, wheeling dragonkites high high
high above blue musselshell and moon—

let waves reach you here, wash salt into
your banded hair, untidy you with secrets—

for they will—

Subduction Zone

faultlines beside us, the Juan de Fuca plate
   offshore, seismologists warning:
              The Big One,
              still to come—

(blue tarps stretch wide
     over houses 'built to code'
         but missing overhang, and rotting,

(an old guy with black lab and
     stale-date takeaway,
         curls up in front of the LCB—

(dumpster-binners, a clutch of women in downtown
     doorways, a toss of squatting street kids
         watch out for the users—

                toxi-
                city

not *The Best Place on Earth*, no,
   for all the ads and lotos-eaters:

         a city of spring and fall,
         about to bloom, on the edge of decay:

tremors,
         underground—

Pinions

The crows know:

the lines they perch on
                              just before night
arrange their coming,
                    the order of departure—

Before the dark claims them with silence,
before their wings flare and fold one last astonishment,
their talons grip them upright, stark
                    silhouettes against the sun—

Downtown,
the gallery steps fill with protest:
          placard-holders rise in tiers, hector, hand
                    pamphlets out and urge petition.

On the sidewalk,
three hawkers twist wire into beaded stickpins—
                              letters, feathers, stars—
              and offer passersby
                    a chance to buy their names—

Cob and Pen

Dockside, yellow gantries manhandle goods
as though tonnage were swan's-weight: *grapple,*

pivot, glide (mechanical birds, feeding their floating
young), *let go*, as though effortless—as though

no caution got in their way, no reprimand,
derision, blush, blunder, rule: bogs and
eddies, storms and slack tides.

On the pier, watching as cargo ships pull out,
I guess at what the blue containers hold—wheat

for the hungry, potash for meagre fields, cobs
of coal for busy mills that send back steel, smoke,

spangles. Tugs ply back and forth. Grey tankers,
slick with oil, dip to the plimsoll line, ease
under the Lion's Gate and fathom distance.

Halfling cygnet, I do not command the gantry's
motherboard, nor steer a cosy luxury

of space: I carry breakbulk on board, foxed
freight and boxed beatitudes: wire fencing

rolled so tight it almost hides the emptiness
I use it for, fixing lines on water, pitching
canvas on the pilings of time—

Square Root

What I remember about the wolf cubs:
The cenotaph in Victory Square, black
armbands under black skies. Military
brass belting orders out, *Taps* in the pelting

rain. Then silence: the bugler, the company
of uniforms. Hat veils and serge overcoats
shuffling grief, fatigue. Compliance. Grim
salutes and grimmer prayers—for peace, king, and

DYB DYB DYB the young: the urge to high-tail it.
Hymns slow enough to send foxholes back to
sleep, and poetry discharging: *torches, triumph,*
sacrifice, death—victory times victory—

something, breath. Marking time, till troop's turn
to lay a drenched wreath below the marble
carving: IS IT NOTHING TO YOV. ALL YE WHO PASS
BY. *Akela*, we say, two fingers peaked

at the brim of our caps, the cloth sodden
green, *We'll DOB DOB DOB,* and are done. Standing
easy, tossing poppies onto the white steps.
Standing by, till DIS-*missed.* The last word.

What I say I forget. Absence. Blood.
The birth of ghosts.

Double Talk

those who think number equals proof:
those who dress in uniform for safety:
those who think mass proves unity:
those who flee the normalcy of difference:
those who think force equals strength:
those who eat fear as if propaganda made it true:
those who accept, believing Authority must outweigh
        thoughtful dissent:
those who dissent because Authority must always be wrong:
those who think easier equals better:
those who say that complicated must be better still:
those who resist the chaos of creativity:
those who equate renewal with dispossession:
those who think *The way I remember* is the same as *The way
        it was*:
those who cannot breathe without a mirror:

two stories going on, the *Sun*, the *Province* alternating:

Comic Strip

Like us, the *funny papers* were at war,
or us because of them, prowling the vacant
lots for trenches to safeguard or treasure
to seize: we became Mandrake on the back
streets of crime, The Asp in the shadows
with Lothar near, or Terry in tropical
colour, fending off marauding pirates—
our sisters, orphaned to Warbucks, were
saved by us, on a generous day.

Everything depended on which paper
we spread in full on the Saturday floor—
the *Province*'s *Prince Valiant* promised
old-time nobility and faithful servants,
the *Sun* leaned towards American jungles
and blonde men named Steve. Miss Twiddle
we knew: she lived on all our blocks,
an interfering busybody. The Dragon Lady
confused us, we didn't yet know why.

Nor did we understand our parents, who laughed at
Gasoline Alley and *Alley Oop*, told us spinach would
make us strong, thrust *Mary Jane & Sniffles*
before us, as though saccharine frolic would satisfy
our lust for elsewhere and escapade. Some of us
turned into teachers, nurses, engineers. Some
joined gangs. We all got 2-way wrist radios and
learned for sure that magnetism controls the universe.
Only one I know of lost an eye.

Xmas Crackers

When is a sailor not a sailor?
    When he's a board.

When is a snowman not a snowman?
    When he's a drift.

When will a poem not be a poem?
    When it's averse.

When will a line not be a line?
    When it's Main Street.

Main Street

Words on signposts totter aloud like peg-
legged birds in alder scrub, drawing stalkers
away from their nests, piping misdirection:
for I see MAIN but hear *ocean*, which colours
how I read the city—

somewhere along the line, maybe I'd heard of
Captain Quadra, maybe seen too many *picture
shows*—Hook, Blood, Sinbad, Kidd—I got
doubloons and the *Spanish* Main, pirates over-
lapping civic history, not altogether off the mark:

From the beginning, margin matters,
city fathers drawing a line on the earth:
they call it *False Creek Road*, join Hastings town
to plank and privateer, eyes on the loggers' camp
at the edge of the slough, the rough sawmill
where fortunes rise and fall:

a rocky ride at the best of times, wheels
sinking in the map and muddy season,
trunk and traveller tossed like ballast:

at least the horses know the way, south,
from below Water Street, roped to port

(*Listen: do you hear dugout canoes at
Luck-Lucky, red cedar and salmon; hear the
ruffle of waves, hawsers straining on three-mast*

ships, white canvas mainsail flaked: do you see
coal aboard, and whole trees?)—

Aldermen retag the road *Westminster*
when wagon ruts grind on to the capital
(parroting London: dreaming large),
and then *Main Street* because, on a patchwork
grid, a *thoroughfare* sounds cosmopolitan:
speculators urge them on, the sea behind them:

though it's not yet a demarcation zone,
more a gravel thumbprint
blurring like Barbary
into the bush:

Speculation

South Vancouver (separate then)
once put the Church Party in power,
some fear of Wobblies and Reds
espousing Prohibition

(*I imagine garrulous Gassy Jack*
rotating in his grave—not much
trepidation there, I'll wager: one or two
preachers among his clientele)

though never any problem buying beer,
no border guards on the streetcar:
fortunes were made on Property
and running rum: *Mi casa es*

Yours, if the price is right? (Voters
tossed the party at the next poll.)

String

During the war, my mother saved string, wound
sisal and butcher's twine into a ball as though
tethering the past to keep tomorrow secure—
proverbs ran her day, *a stitch in time, idle
hands, a cat may look at a king*—reserving
space for salt and superstition: *white rabbits,*
she'd whisper as each month rolled around,
then look up, laugh, *time to put the kettle on—*

One of the city's new parks is called Tea Swamp,
another's named for Major Matthews, the old man
who clipped whatever he believed important
out of the local papers—scandals, strikers, social
elites: famous visitors and August Jack: if he'd lived
longer, he'd have dredged up placards against Expulsion,
the needle exchange, Winter Games, another war,
worked out who strung who along, and gathered why—

Time warp: on the school grounds I used to watch
Harvey Lowe, the yo-yo man, *pushing the line,*
looping *around the world* while standing still
(and me awkward, *over the moon*, tangled
in string that would not dance *cat's cradle*)—

Step along Main, or drift down side streets, into
jazz clubs, temples, pool halls, parks, an archive's
sleeping there, who knows what you'll find—
physics, faith, a lucky cup of leaves—the
string we hold, the rabbits we chase, the bog
and bits of history we choose to call true—

Boggers

In alder scrub at the city's canted edge, an hour's walk
from where I call home, Camosun Bog lies hidden
from parable and passers-by—

no wulvers here, no kelpies to care for the rain,
no elves in trees or trolls beneath the bridges—sprites,
pixies, missing, gone (lean cat-tail stalks spin
all on their own into overnight gold: and coyotes,
scrabble-thin, are hunting game)—

On the weekend, the neighbourhood transforms: sudden
down-to-earth cryptographers gather bogside to uproot
ivy, knotweed, rusting cans and sprawling archangel:

they nudge muddy dump to moss-fed pond, sing
blackbird songs, plant difference in place of discard—

street by street, the city grows—

Grade

At six I thought if I climbed into the cab of
old Engine 374 I could see the whole world,
and I could: Kits Beach up close, the Sleeping
Beauty farther off: in my head I was already
through the next range and the one after,
out of the spiral tunnel, over the top,
free pass to beyond—

Everywhere the world dazzled, the way
early snow lights up a mountain peak, insisting
we climb: branched apple trees and cedar
poles, linesmen's spikes reaching high:
fir trees higher: pictures in *Life*—Eiffel,
Everest, Empire State, all claiming *highest*—
temptation, invitation—

The big draw at the PNE—no, I can't
say that: for some it was the livestock,
4-H piglets, Guernsey calves: for others
the Big Dipper, Midway spieling, fancy
peelers and free food—for me, the Shoot-the-
Chute: that long ladder up, the breathless drop,
high summer splashing—

So quick, the fall.
We played musical chairs in Grade One,
dodgeball later on: learning to win perhaps—

scrambling for the only life raft, attacking
the weakest first—or taught to lose?

Survival: someone was always being
tossed off the train.

We marvelled when Hilary *conquered* Chomo-
lungma, had to focus to remember Tenzing
who showed him the way.   Now everyone
expects to summit Everest. Though maybe the
snow is soft, the ice edge brittle. Number 374
should have taught us that. The hard part
is climbing down.

Hedges

walk shaughnessy: walk
southwest marine:

walk the narrow lots of kits and
collingwood, notice the hedges—cedar   privet
                                   holly laurel
                                          yew:
four-feet, twenty-feet: what do you
see:
        you get used to not seeing,
peering through scratch and tangle

        (the wonder of what's hidden:
                cachet:
                        suspicion):

walk the metrics of the line, be
ready for anything, spittle, good will, brash
interruption: unhinged gate, junked chevy,
dry white tripping sea of flatfish plastic bags:

first rule of escape: avoid
        eye contact: pretend you belong,
        have someplace to go, an entrance:

as though you expected welcome, even
round the back,
        (ivy,
        frost,
        old clothes):

Disposed

Surveyors built 'Champlain Heights'
    on top of the old city dump—
        what's in a name—golf greens sitting now
          where bedsteads used to mound,
            ashcans,
            pots,
            broken bones, men
        crawling over them,
        burning.
                Suburbs of good cheer.

Does smoke still swirl on the 14th tee,
do leg bones turn on the spit,
Royal City tins rise ragged on the
    playground's edge,
        ready to rip, spring-
          loaded?

The order of surfaces:
        automated trucks,
        curbside collections,
        disposal somewhere else, removed
        out of sight.   In-
        cineration bays.
            The sound of rubbish,
            science of spill.

Open the garbage can: finger
    history—spoiled chicken,

smoking notes,
games for two in plastic boxes,
uncapped anger,
rusty lies, torn expec-
tations,
pampering—

We are not disposed to.

Castaways.

Puzzle pieces scatter in the alley:
dried roses, *Hi my name is,*
hunger—

Main Street

At Pender Street, a red and gold lion dances
right through the intersection—

tin drums and rattles, smoke and BANG-BANG-BANGING
warning the devils KEEP AWAY:

>   (*Tourists sample the souvenir shops,*
>   *hang about the steam clock, Gassy Jack's statue*)

No way of telling where the devils are hiding,
under an awning at the prawn-seller's, yawning
in gaps below the clam-and-oyster stalls, noise
the fire-tiger's breath, the dragon's yaw, the lion's
rolling infinity billowing the street:

>   (*The old people remember other days:*
>   *head tax, exclusion acts, the knotweed talk*
>   *of opium dens and YELLOW PERIL:*
>
>   *during the riots,*
>   *police were quick to draw lines*)

The lion drums devils into distance:
until the loudest sound's the pitch of wind-chime:

glass-paper

leaf-wrinkle
rain:

Edge of the Map

at the edge: land
    slipping into sea, the country slumping,
        into everything, nothing,
            where the world ends:

Hey—I already know what others laugh at,
    early morning runs around the sea wall,
        bandanna wrapped tight against the rain:
    mid-morning cappuccino on the upper terrace,
        the one with the better view: late morning
    latte: on skis by noon:
                drifting

    past the idea of work into afternoon tea on the rolling
    lawn or pot smoke in the sleepy square, nothing
    else to do, rolled-up sidewalks and ebbing tide—

But I am HERE, not
        'OUT THERE': *slow*
             up—
                  Listen,
the rhythm, the blue edge leading:

out-of-time zone, sing
west of Boundary, sing
where I live, its sea-leap
        syllables:
                at the edge
plankton begins, the guts and bones of high
hope, Raven-song, the pond blood of
cranberries—

Outside In

high ceiling and *sea floor,*
door to the Orient, window on the world:

we build to let the outside in, haul
   depth and height out of the far sublime
      and into living room:

it's Elsewhere that plays *keep away,*
   turns *All Those Mountains* into a wall—

for us they're where we walk
     and who we walk with,
   how we find where rivers meet the sky,
     settle the arrogant dust
       of straight lines—

low ceiling:
the mountains disappear,
   Grouse and Hollyburn
     vanish, Seymour becomes an oxy-
      moron, the lower world
       closes in:

   colour here
     an Onley landscape:
   Erickson's concrete
     grey against grey—

we know downpour, drizzle,
thunder along the mountains, the grammar
of cloud and timing:

    my favourite forecast:
        scattered showers,
        changing during the day
        to occasional rain—

the hundred words for dampness:
    moss
    bay
    sound
    sea
    bog
    bight
    saltchuck
    slough—

the delta drowned,
   the North Shore reeling,
     June,
     November,
     more of the same—

Had you been here last week,
   we tell the tourists,
you could have seen forever: eden
   a function of *if it were clear,*
subjunctive
   rainbow-eyed—

Reel Story

But you want the real story:

    right—it's midnight Friday, early Saturday
        morning, maybe rain, maybe no rain,
five hundred people—more—mostly
        young, 20s anyway, late teens—roaming
           up and down Granville Mall,
        twos, tens,
        louder with the night, grabbing
        japadog & fries, falafel from a
        fast-food wagon, another beer at
        one of the new hotels, just the
           old hotels with new names,
           same women, same beer, and
        one more stop at the money mart—

night reporters out mining other stories, some
        gang rape, firebug, bashing—
        somewhere in the city someone's
off their meds,
        down a blind alley buying speed for the
        first time, last time, someone's
sleeping, someone's
dying, someone's
pacing 'cos their kid's not home and it's
        already 3, someone's
calling cops, someone's
hiding from the light, Hyperion, Lucifer,
        Archangel Raphael, someone's
deep in conversation, listening, joking,
        laughing choking

weeping retching
lying awake with the television on, watching
the shopping network, *new uses for plastic
wrap,* someone's
running, someone's reaching, someone's
starting out a just new day, yawning, stretching, plodding
down the hill to a Starbuck's coffee, someone's
ending a late shift, padding round the Safeway looking
for chicken soup and
low-fat ice cream,
walking driving
jogging biking
shouting screwing
baking rye or frying eggs or
stirring bouillabaisse, someone's
giving birth, someone's
scrambling a jigsaw, someone's
finishing a mystery, practising a tenor sax, slow
dancing on a quiet beach, lying un-
conscious on the front porch, someone's
talking muffled to themselves, am-
biguous as turnips,

waiting in the dark for a bus that never comes, screaming

help me,

this is my city,

I am here—

Track

How we tell tales: in cycles, sagas; set lines and
footprints; exaggerating, understating,
chancing a big payoff, tracking our lives (how we
chase beauty, count acquisition), *twenty to one*—

Thoroughbreds at Hastings Park race blinkered round
an oval, hold the fence from barred stall to finish line,
maybe headshot, red rose horseshoe, trifecta stubs
cashed in, torn—all or nothing, *either/or*—

We speak in threes—gods, people, possibilities:
three score and ten, how many makes a crowd, *two boys
are half a boy and three boys are none*—mouthing
certainties but seeking *both/and*, the clear unclear—

go figure—and read by trees: Ornamental cherries
hemming the city's boulevards, the numbered avenues;
rows of maples wearing the elegance of arbor,
budding, blazing, shedding. Though tree stories end

in elder, ash, casting the paradox of calculated
shade. Horse chestnuts hurl crows in nesting season,
hurtle conkers like insults and stern birthdays; a
cypress arm strikes; an overhang of holly snatches—

but tired walkers seldom stop to listen: con-
strained by regimen, they tear ahead, pretend to be
detached, nagged by how far they've come, how far to go
before the next corner. City workers
cruise the clogged drains, inhalators
stall in the roundabouts—

And Yet

the untidy energy of sea and sky,
    nothing lasts for long:

try standing rigid on Granville Island—im-
    possible, activity dis-
       rupts, engages: coffee
corrugates the air, talk
    steams into every crevice,
Ocean trucks roll thunder out of
    limestone mix and sand, cedar
Haida masks carve transformation—

even the market stacks of Okanagan apples—
    Granny Smith, Ambrosia—shine
      fire-fierce, like oncoming
        laughter, like *not now, not yet, soon*
          earthquake, avalanche—

and on the water, women in dragonboats
    pull *Stroke Stroke Stroke*
                forward: they are
survivors, rowing: sharing their stories to refuse
    drowning, achieving something in-
      tangible, im-
        possible—

In Camera

That moment before the steam clock blasts noon,
no time exists: even the tourists' eyes
are shutterless, no muscle flexes, no
shuffle agitates the sea they stand on.

In front of the Aquarium, Bill Reid's whale
holds forever balanced on its tail fin—Chief
of the Undersea World. Off Chestnut Street, a
steel crab shines stainless, polishes still.   On

Locarno beach, volleyball players pause in mid-
serve, -spike, -dig. Nothing moves until the mind,
supposing *if,* clicks *yet, next, now,* the rip of
history, the moon-ride *then*—

Main Street

Where Main crosses Hastings used to be
the centre of town, columns and cupola:

now it's the edge—poverty, trafficking,
lines of powder, tales of abuse:

Has some people carrying on, who don't see
past gaunt corners, don't listen to those who live
in the *Downtown East Side,* won't learn
history:

A concrete viaduct stretches overtop:

> *I was nine the first time I climbed aboard*
> *a Great Northern train, rattled south from the*
> *Main Street station all the way to White Rock—*
> *fished salmon streams and bullhead ponds*
> *and the endless barnacled pier—I only ever*
> *heard about Hogan's Alley—*

SIN CITY to some (who figured the
   Harlem Nocturne stripped more than jazz
   back to bass and bare trombone),

JAZZ STREET to others (sweet blue horn, tremo-
   low), Jimi's grandma's street, and that

African
Methodist
Episcopal Fountain Chapel sang out
Promise with the gospel *Hallelu,*
say

HOME to the porters, their wives, their children:
ran angled off Jackson, in behind the
Main Street storefronts, Union to Prior:

> *I'd seen the men before, aboard the train,*
> *but didn't ask, didn't think to ask,*
> *didn't know I didn't know—*

their houses demolished for the viaduct:

some talked of rapture, the world to come:

Moss

grows underfoot, spreads
   up and down the north bark of trees, tells you
      acid's in the soil, dampness,
         umbrage in the
            dark latitude of winter—

people here spray anti-moss on trees, nail
   zinc along the shadow side of shingles, dance
      antic on grease-slick sidewalks, they are
        galvanized by
           sightings in the lawn—

Look for the mountains, that's North
                (the mountains are invisible
  in stray fog and grey rain,
                    every
     way is north, the trees
        encased in moss, the air
           sluggish, heavy, soft)—

Salt

sea:

surrounds us,
    washes the gritty sand, the pebble
        beaches, clay at Jericho—
            (Jerry's Cove, once:
            no chorus of horns)

walk by the grasslands there,
    green willows weep along old creek paths,
        tough chicory holds to the hardscrabble edge,
          the ocean stills—

walk away and the sea follows:
    the air damp
        and sundown windshift cooling—

           red hydrants mark
           where hoses can tap into water,
           where afterdark film crews concoct rain—
           blue hydrants say sea:
           the firefighters' sign of a saltwater pool:

we carry clay with us,
    pebbles in our boots,
        coast unforgotten:

naked as Wreck Beach
    in a hot high summer, we carry
        salt in case of an eastwind snow—

2. REHEARSAL

Sunset, Sunrise, Shannon, Strathcona,
Rupert, Renfrew, Fleming, Winona—

Carnarvon, Killarney, Quilchena, Connaught,
Callister, Crowley, Cook, Chaldecott—

Woodland, Wainborn, Vanier, Victoria,
Riley, Rogers, Ross, Pandora—

Grandview, Riverview, Fraserview, Tea,
Malkin, Memorial South, Moberly—

Lost

Something so simple as
ball hockey in the back lane,

walking the dog along a
huckleberry path off Crown
or Camosun,

something so simple as seagulls,
the young grey ones
or the harried old whitewings:

what have I stopped noticing?

> the impatient shout
> *Car!* —

> the stretch of leash at the startle of
> junco or torpid raccoon—

> the order of calling at the
> quickening rush of an onshore squall—

>> complex lines of connection,
>> dependency.

I am caught up in tangle,
fishnets of caution, repetition:

where has the moment gone, single
featherstroke, sudden

berryblush,
vermilion cheek and child hurrah—

voices—
     fixed forever

and then—
     dropped in fogbank,
     murmured into approximation,
     lost, like
     willow play and grey signs—

Play

I mean, listen to the children—
the laughing giddy rapid chatter rising on the wind,
loud, then loud again,
blocks away from any elementary school:

    the buzzer goes, and then, seconds later,
    clamour—

it's not just any noise:
it could be yelling *Go go go*,
it could be talking *didjasee* and *thenshesaid*, it could be
crying, stifled in a sleeve, it could be laughing
kookaburra songs,

    random as salmonberries —

hubbub:
it's the forest, the leafy
revelry, stem and root, where

    one tree grows, amazing,
    one tree more,

we saw it as a sapling, then we say, *yes*—

but did we?
play, I mean,
or listen to the leaving?

I am

On a patch of plain grass
    at 14th and Pine,
a young man lifts a bagpipe
    onto his shoulder,
      straightens,
        fits lips on the chanter.

A starting note sounds, swells
            Carry the lad
out of isolation into memory,
    the air reverberating.
           Over the sea—

At the end of the park,
    a lone far block along,
      a pilot-capped child
      climbs aboard a swing, leans
        back, leans
            forward, gathers
      impetus to soar towards the sky.

No-one else is near.

    I am that man singing
      reeds at the sun.

The one walking by.

The single child still.

Boom

Follow Angus south of Marine,
or Barnard, the river comes at you
silent, one minute grass, the next
browncurrent surging—

Hold to the dike, it will protect you,
you will not drown, you tell yourself,
not this time, not yet, not today—

Time was: not here but by the
mudshore east of Ross, out from the
NO SWIMMING sign, scribbled on and
pried almost off its treetrunk post—
but who at ten would read the signs:

    didn't look rough, that water,
    didn't look fast, deep,
    didn't look far,
        berryscrub edge to one of the booms—

    massive they were, those peelbark
        logs, the scent of the cut still
            sharp in the nostrils, a lumber yard
                not far away,
    massive, waiting for
        downriver swing, and
  silent, chained, inviting,
      balance
            already real in the head: to dance
                  athletic on top of the floating world—

sudden, the rolling,
      pulling apart, back, not a word
      down, and anything with:
                                    just

      a slip of a thing. Nothing

            personal—

Bridge

on sky hooks, my mother said,
where we stretched to hang dreams—

I imagined the Lions Gate to hang there too,
steel cables pirouetting into clouds,

arcs of impossible lightness
reaching past earth's edges:

not disappointed when I learned
it was Guinness instead that held it up:

one pint or two, I asked:
no, not disappointed—

dreams have a way
of finding a path to ground—

Main Street

runs a beeline south from Hastings
along the flats and up the hill to where
Kingsway angles off towards New West:

I used to take the #7 streetcar the other
way: north into town, up Fraser past
Govier's, Houghland's, the Imperial Bank,
McBain's and Buckerfield's, Cunningham's, Macphail's,
past Hilton's Dairy and the five and dime, past
Mountain View (angels, pebbles,
David's star), past all the mission halls
and the fundamentals:

screech left at Kingsway (the monocled
Aristocrat doffed his top hat
and twirled his neon cane), then
rattle down Main past the old hotels,
already seedy before I knew
what seediness implied: *Cobalt, Ivanhoe*:

I heard Normans, Saxons, swords and bows,
saw the Steller's jay of a January sky:

Later I worked at the Avon,
though I missed the night the cops raided
Tobacco Road.

Two sides to everything, people said:

Two sides to Main:

Mountain View

We are born into
    wood sea fire metal stone

Where we lay our head
    stencilled onto a burning sidewalk

Sails tack and billow

Roofbeams couple in the touching sky

Wire fences rust, are tossed aside
    till moss bog swallows them

Mottled granite
    fastens us to sleep

Trunk

Ads trumpeted abroad the new *Dominion*
Tower, Tallest Building in the Empire,
promised circular stairs at the southeast
corner, marble, white: all the verities
and a stellar view—

So they came for the work, out of India and
unemployed on the Christchurch Downs:
my grandfather still young, his firstborn a boy,
his Cockney wife whom I never knew
square-jawed against the unimaginable—
.

distance, time—what more unlikely than
all those days at sea, the trek by train—
maybe only the mansard Tower itself,
orange-yellow-red, *Second Empire*
in a wash of colonial grey—

They built a home at the far end of scrub,
him carrying lumber on his shoulders,
thirty blocks down Main Street, I can only
imagine the military gait, the tons of coal
and cords of fir that fed the furnace:

> *I see her in a black-and-white photograph,*
> *unsmiling, laced Victoria, and him in*
> *uniform, solemn beside her, standing correct,*
> *as stubborn as habit, raising Canadians—*
>
> *I think of them now for daring to grow: him*
> *as fierce as grit on a marble wall but willing*

to climb those stairs to the far Dominion sky,
EK, DO, TEEN, CHAR, *a map in his hand of*
what he could see, and her holding tight to a
CROWDED-SPACE *of nightingales—*

Dancing

On a giddy day—didn't matter the season,
crayon rays or liquid sunshine—my parents
would dance the Charleston in the middle of
the kitchen: hold their knees, twist their heels,
kick out their feet, *shimmy shake shake shake*—

I laughed, flung limbs about as though joining in—
but not long after turned away, learned alley
attitude and tuned in to the long decade I shared
with my friends, somewhere between *Don't
Fence Me In* and Joni paving paradise.

They didn't understand, we said: we were in
love: all April we wore blue suede on our feet,
and brushing aside the old linoleum stood
hangdog on the corner, many-splendoured,
waiting for someone who'd say *Only you,*

Put your head on my shoulder, someone who
might even listen if we dared *I get ideas*,
maybe Donna, Diana, Little Susie, Peggy Sue:
they shook us up, we rocked the clock,
the decade ended.

Another began, though we scarcely noticed,
so pressed for time: we settled for the moment
with our one-and-only—Rita, Rigby, Jude or
Maggie Mae—sometimes hard, those days,
penny-lonely when we told the sunshine goodbye,

but we had some help from our friends, learned
the words to parenthood, played carpenter and
walrus and danced on the kitchen floor, twist and
shout. Suddenly the children didn't understand,
wanted to move to moonwalk, Chilliwack, Overdrive:

Noise, we said, and next we knew they'd moved.
We weren't ready: the silence paralyzed—
how high the moon climbed without our noticing,
how shadows echoed, only absence rapping at the
door. We stumbled when the radio played *oldies*

and we knew the words, recognized the rhythm.
Out we walked into April rain, wondering where
the corner was: found ourselves humming along,
tapping our feet when the Charleston returned.
Love, we said, the place we live, it's all singing.

We sing with the little ones now, *Wheels on the
bus, You are my sunshine*. They laugh, wave their
arms about, wriggle onto the floor, draw pictures
of happy suns in rainbow crayon. From the next
room, we hear even the ceiling dancing—

Listen

silence in the city—
a time so distant only bees seemed loud
and miles south and east of Hallelujah Point,
the 9 o'clock gun clapped
                    I MEAN IT:
brittle curfew,
into summer bush and gullied play—

      Noise now every minute, gunning shrieking
      grumbling idling
      screaming droning
      sputtering whining

        boombox and cell—

am I lost in listening-land?

          no grass grows quietly long,
          no ripe forest's left to fall—

        Call
        curfew—

No: I would not be deaf to the city,
its sibilant stutter, klaxon caterwaul,

only to play the gaps
          and intervals, still
hear when small children chirp discovery,
make time for the mason bees—

Sliding

omigod,
  sliding down
    Trimble Hill, the speed the
   straight down
    daring
     neverstop
     unthinking
      joy of just
      doing it,
        consequence
        beyond reason,
       crash
        unimagined,
        unabatable,
       the moment
       flying,
       fast
       faster
        stretching into
        oversnow and
         wintertumble,
          wingtrick and cold
          cantilever,
           eyebright,
            air_____

Ice

One of those rare years,
minus-nine for ten days straight, the sun low
and bright and ice-fog drifting in and out of
cedar fronds, Lost Lagoon slowly freezing:

>*is it safe yet, can I skate yet,*

the children, unused to ice outside the indoor rink—

No joy for birds: the swans puzzled, food scarce,
their rush nests stiff with angularity: in the black
chestnut branches, crows auguring

>*Caution,*
>*Catastrophe,*

and down on the ice, random geese
skidding across the unfamiliar—

Day ten   fifteen centimetres   sudden colour:

Pond ice scrambling with children, their skates still

>*hi hi hi*

nickel bright from the Army & Navy, scarves, tuques,
mittens, parkas red as Township maple
loud against the conifers,

>*Watch me, Watch,*
ankles bending in, hockey stick a tripod, *Watch*

ME,

parents' eyes racing, counting numbers, testing
weight, calculating   fastest rushing distance
frozen fountain to blue-grass shore—

one of those rare years: and then
                                        overnight,
                crocuses bursting purple,
                swans piloting SLOW NORMAL,
                parents home again in rain gear—
                only the crows still calling *Caution*—

Down on the ground the children laughing, chasing
soccer balls, lighting again upon their baseball gloves,
tucking away the ice on Lost Lagoon for a day they
do not picture yet, when they'll remember,
out of nowhere,
                one of those years—

Field of Play

We talked of trading *All-Wheat* cards,
   the latest escapades of Superman,
      The Shadow Knows,
         radio was king,
         our fathers next,
         and older brothers off to war—

Competition: over who could do what—
   kick, catch, throw, collect—
   and what our fathers did:
      why it mattered
      more than all the others,
      older brothers off to war—

Building houses, says one:
 keeps the trains rolling:
   stevedore at the sugar dock,
      and that sounded sweet,
      but no-one asked
      what a stevedore was—

Workmen all.
  No-one's father
    drummed or danced or sang—
      though years on
      when competition for the Best Girl
      took over, we were glad of a

drummer and the Commodore's
  sprung floor. Our older brothers, some of them,
   returned, preaching

French sugar, foreign spies, and
roll-your-own Paree
we thought them

glamorous,
　or condescending:　　and so
　　danced our way past them, we thought,
　　　　and way beyond our fathers,
　　　　into what mattered,
　　　　what we settled on—

We don't meet any more,
　don't trade e-mails or green stamps or
　　birthday cards or shouts at the Legion.
　　　　Out There, in broom and ivy,
　　　　our fathers rest, our older brothers
　　　　dance with shadows.

Schooling

Tempting to read the phone book as an epic, every cat-
egory in the yellow pages a catalogue of heroes: Take the
schools—

Britannia,
Byng, Lord
Churchill, Sir Winston
David Thompson
Gladstone
Hamber, Eric
John Oliver
Killarney
King George
Kitsilano
Magee
Point Grey
Prince of Wales
Templeton
Tupper, Sir Charles
University Hill
Vancouver Technical
Windermere

—ignore the erratics of the phone company's order, every
school's an alpha to those who lead the cheers—*Pericles
Sophocles Peloponnesian War: French verbs Latin verbs
H_2SO_4: We're for the strong side . . . the right . . . Fight*—
memory's martial corners lit by the politics of assumption

—maybe the most imperial names have lost their old
resonance, maybe they've been washed thin in the ragged
wake of history—but march them together on dry land,
they still wear scraps of an old uniform: motley now, the
collars less tight, some of the jacket buttons undone.

—I haven't forgotten even yet all the old rhymes from
elementary days—*The 24th of May is the Queen's Birth-day,
if you don't give us a holiday,* Maypole dances, the girls
in ringlets and boys lined up along the sidelines—they
tried to keep us sitting in rows even in secondary school,
though anarchy rustled
  behind the bike shed and
    under the bleachers. Nothing
      wrong with a
        wise selective
        memory,
          growing
           here—

Cleavage

Railway posters sometimes graced the walls in grade school—
or Hudson's Bay calendars?—*illustrations*, not *paintings*, no
mention of Shadbolt or Carr—

and for all we goggled at movie ads by day, Venus would
never raise her arms in the locked schoolroom.

But when the Blue Boy opened at the foot of the hill, where
old Moberly Annex used to lean,

we learned that *pitchers* were hung in beer parlours, too, not
just schools and churches. *In facsimile*.

Constable. Rockwell.
Venus for sure.
Goya. *Saturno*
devorando a su hijo.

We learned later about the peeler clubs on Main: St. Regis,
Nocturne, things that adults whispered when they dropped
the face they usually wore with *little pitchers* near:

jokes that some men laughed at when they said *No cover*
charge—

As for art, it took years to split a kind of fact from many
kinds of fiction, stop eating our own—

Main Street

Get close to the False Creek flats (reclaimed land,
dredged up from the sea) and soon I'm running
on memory tracks, Yaletown, railway terminals,
CN, GN, a roundhouse of confusion:

(is it true? that when I was a kid
we bought vegetables from the Premier's father?)

yes, on Powell: though he wasn't the Premier then,
scarcely older than I was, and I used to call his father
the banana man—he'd walk about his barn of a shop,
stop and talk, hand out food to all the children while
parents circled potato stalls:

I learned talk might take you anywhere—
can't leave this city without crossing bridges:

(my city uncles knew False Creek well,
butcher, sawyer, cooper, welder:
knew it was never a creek, at best a saltwater
slough—mostly factory sludge before it cleaned up
into sailboat harbour)

Yaletown's all condos now, Strathcona gentrified,
a seawall separates the flats from the sea:

The two bridges you can't see from Creek's end—
eight-laned Granville, fast and sleek,
art-deco Burrard, with the airless city motto on its
arch, *By sea and land we prosper*—they still wear

the gloss of boardroom
more than the beltswing of union:

(no easy leap from Eastside west
in early days: direction
not the only false border to cut across)

you leave tracks,
even on infill:

Machine Man

I remember the machine shop my father worked in,
the bench with the single bulb overhead,
the whine as his lathe whirred slower, the men shouting
hand signals, noise an occupying army
on the work floor,

> *hoist-rattle,*
> *hammerclank,*
> *crash*:

I remember
the cuts on my father's face, the broken nose
unshaped by flying metal—the hands
washed gentle
      but never free from oilcan grime—
the power his strong arms had
to lift more than engines—

> *steel shavings on the benchtop,*
> *heavy trays on makeshift shelves,*
> *solder, bolts, rivets, rethread screws,*
> *and on the floor his open toolbox,*
> *clamps, pliers, drivers, cutters,*
> *drillbits, wrenches, ball peen, chain—*

Engine surgeon, he could fix almost anything.

> *Almost, I say,*
> *Aladdin at the cave.*

I remember laughter,

I remember

the deafness that wrapped him later
in silent rooms—

Disorder

I no longer remember the order of things.

Was the summer we spent a week
  in a tumbledown shack in Fisherman's Cove
    before
      or after
        the time we took the Galloping Oilcan
          from Steveston port to Sidney marina—

and did adolescence take place on
  this side of reality
    or the other, it can be hard to tell:
      the moon is blue.

Numbers unreliable,
  Dimensions mislead—

What you hadn't counted on hides
  always unexpected round a
    corner you didn't know you'd reached
      in the middle of a grid:

      The West End is full of them:
      Dead ends—

Do we seek gridlock, thinking it
  secure?

The streets are already rebelling.

They change their names,
  they disappear like ghosts,
    they want us lost, like
      broken toys in long grass until the
      lawnmower coughs overhead,
      their secret wish is
          tumbledown—

Main Street

at the edge of the Creek I've seen thousands
gather on a summer night, watch fireworks
bloom like poppies:

or placards aloft, march, run to demonstrate
for, against, because:

or go about their day:

    a tough slog uphill
    from here to Mount Pleasant—

    sirens screaming vermilion,
    traffic a tangle of firethorn,
    cars trucks bikes buses criss-
    crossing, radi-
    ating,
    wires strung over-
    head like
    netting

    (schools nearby, *David Livingstone,*
    Florence Nightingale, General Brock,
    tethered to heritage, one register)—

above the flats and latticed railway yards,
the old blocks afford an unsettled view,
houses mainly two up, two down, Arts &

Crafts, Edwardian: wooden fire ladders
clutch the siding—

in a downpour of dark, there's no sleep
for those on the edge: young painters, pipers,
actors, writers clambering the landings,
setting off light in an attic of signs:

Disconnect

You recognize those born here
by how they pronounce the city's name,
    Vang-COO-ver,
    never *VaN-kew-ver,*
that's the voice of national tv, the idiom of
Elsewhere, the *cric* sound of pre-recorded
voicemail, disconnect—

but talk to oldtimers and sooner or later
you'll hear the local syllables: they'll start
eulogizing Woodward's—hum the $1.49 Day
jingle, nostalgia washing over them—their eyes
will glaze and suddenly they'll blurt

    Tuesday, once-a month,
    My mother useta buy everythin' there.
    Ballpoint pens. Woodrose cups. New
    underpants. We still got some in the
    basement. Cups I mean. For the cabin,
    if we ever would've had one, which we don't.
    Or the kids, who say No Thanks too damn
    quick, or You gotta be Joe King more like,
    some drawl they learned offa some
    I-gadget and anyways they got no idea
    what it means to scrimp 'n save—

    And everyone went, right? Even
    Shaughnessy with hats 'n blue hair
    who wouldn't be caught dead on
    that part of Hastings 'cept for dollar-forty-nine
    or that shoe sale once-a year at the

Army 'n Navy down skid road a bit—
yeah, skid ROAD, not skid ROW—
down where the loggers useta room
when they hit town at the end o' the season—
no-one called 'em lumberjacks in
this neck o' the woods— 'n drank up
the beer parlour next door, eh?—
on the MEN side, right—

Kids these days.   Just hang out at the mall.
Check out the labels.   Got no damn sense—

Needles

think *up* and *down*, not *latitude*—
reach comes later, a consequence of
asphalt and suburb, the idea of *big*
pricking civic aspiration:

imagine a sign on top of the low-rise
Sylvia: DINE IN THE SKY—or a **W**
circling *high* above Woodward's
department store, the *Sun* Tower

· a tower still, babel with a small **b**, no
Shangri-La, no rival for the mountains—

on the ground, imagine fir needles, pine,
wild ginger, bur:

the floor of the five-and-dime
is oiled, not veneered—
buttons, buckles, hooks, pins
fill tidy boxes:

my mother never forgets how
Woolworths refused her a job:
You couldn't see over the counter,
the manager said.

Bridge 2

we see the islands, have even set foot
    on some of them, summer camp, *industrial park*—
        Bowen, Lulu, Mitchell, Iona—
Galiano drifting on the distant ocean, anchoring arbutus
    and the long moment of mackerel sky—

but seldom look down
    at the islands we lace around our ankles,
tie like bollards to wanderlust
    and curiosity—

downtown is an island:
        not red, not green,
each block flashing violence,
    alleys of shadow and yellowsetting sun—

the daring, the danger, of crossing
    out of the familiar, into question, stray,
choosing possibility (laughter/loving:
    mockery/pain)—

the choosing:
    not compelled—
        Being:

Dine in the Sky

Track your way from The Sylvia,
    out of the all-too-comfortable lounge,
    go ahead, call it *snug*,

Track your way along the sea wall, past
    the Alexandra Bandstand, past Joe
Fortes and the hot buttered popcorn stalls
    where the old wharf used to toss
    skinny boys and oversmocked girls into
        giddy English Bay,
past men coupled hand-in-hand and
    women in white shoes trudging slowly home
        from a too-long shift at St. Paul's—

Notice the palm trees, wrapped in burlap against
    the possibility of just-too-cold,

Notice the cargo ships lying offshore,
    waiting for a berth at Terminal Docks, and
    maybe the sun drifting downwards, the sky
    already reddening behind the university,
        prickly silhouette, grey against Grey—
But do not stop:
ahead stands the stone Inukshuk—
    he looks out of place, I used to say,
    once—
        no more—
it is the standing that matters now,
    arms outstretched, reaching—

Here—

3. IN CONCERT

Thunderbird, Delamont, Granville, Nanaimo,
Hillcrest, Kingcrest, Tisdall, Tatlow—

Carleton, Collingwood, Kerrisdale, Clark,
Almond, Columbia, Adanac Park—

bog and ravine, too low or too high:
acreage land-grabbers chose to pass by—

thank accident then for this space to be green in:
turns out to be air we can now try to breathe in—

Flickers

Spring:
    and the annual Territorial starts again,
    squirrels chasing last year's siblings
        out of the apple trees,
    chickadees piping *Ee-oo*
        like tiny rescue wagons,
    flickers pecking *Lookatme Lookatme*
        on every metal gas vent in the city,
          strutting—

No stranger to plumage:
    you still have that flowered shirt you wore
    when Carnaby Street rescued everyone
        from pressed grey, still note when
    chittering miniskirts perch on the corner,
    still feel a smile flit across your face
        and a tumble in your belly—

Not dead yet, old man—no,
    not ready for the box wagon yet—
    those sticks you lean on, in three-leafed
        clover?
        tap out a tattoo—

Inside:
you're chirping—

Keep Looking

So look around: see that young mother
teaching her small daughter, she never
stops teaching her, she never stops
being a mother, years from now she'll
still be asking *Aren't you cold, Have you
had enough to eat,*

today she's saying *Watch out for cars,*
every day training, attention, not
entitlement:
       *Look left, look right, look
           left again,*

and at the corner where the flashing light
flicks on and off, *Look for the man walking,
Listen for the north-south cuckoo, the west-
east churrup* of the automatic birds—

In Fairview, in Grandview,   pause,
      look out across the city:

on a crisp day, the heart feeds on the rise
of distant mountains, one leap and you could
leave the grid, be this instant riding an un-
familiar board, corking a halfpipe,

        the Lions crouching snow-white high
        over Capilano Canyon: cutouts

        dwarfing the towers that scrape
        the lower sky, the urban world pre-
        occupied with pigeons, when

Watch out!
        your mother's voice in your ear,
        the robot whirr of Broadway
                snaps the pipedream cold.

Keep walking west, keep
walking.
                Listen for the birds.
Look up, left, right, look
                                up again,
in case the young snows melt,
the Lions disappear—

Blue Screen

small wonder
features

the blue screen
glances

scenes
reeling

our minds
inventing

back
drop

story
the world

we see
on film

imagined
here

Main Street

Walk, Broadway to King Ed, read
the signs: new life along the strip,
baby shops, sushi, yams, cassava,
vegan, organic, hundred-mile green,
the latest embraces among the young:

REDUCE REUSE RECYCLE's taken over
from CLEAN UP PAINT UP BEAUTIFY:
Car Co-op cars share preselected
spaces (*Alderwood, Sophia,
the IGA*), green energy appeals,
GO CANUCKS GO:

St. Pat's still draws a crowd, largely
Filipino (a mile away *Goldilocks*
sells *ube* cakes): film trucks
come and go, hum invention:

A few blocks west along 12th Avenue,
on a granite plinth, in Roman bronze,
The Captain stands by the back steps
to city hall: George Vancouver, solid
navigator, diplomat in a minor key, no
saint, no hero despite the pose:

he holds a scroll in his hand,
affirming his commission,
and points northeast to the harbour
as though he were still at sea:

Whoi-Whoi or *Brobdingnag?*—
the mapmaker on the line:

that pull between the already cast
and the uncertain coast ahead:

Intersections

Driving Kingsway: where it crosses Victoria, the old Colonial Motel's renamed—a sense of Empire's still strong though, fast food chains on all the corners. Burgers. Donuts. Coffee.

Used to be a carriage road through bush and woodlot, Gassy Jack's Gastown to New West, the Royal City: inns at the overnight stopping points, Cedar Cottage, say—and then secondhand carlots took their place, waving flags. A Day's Inn's there now, Starbucks at the intersections, sometimes kiddie-corner, catching the traffic both ways. Café menus in Thai, Lao, Vietnamese. We feed on signs.

A few corner stores persist, pails of daffodils in front, dollar-ninety-nine for five stems, bread and cigarettes the staples. Used to be Sweet Caps in the window, Crush in the cooler, Malkin's Best or Singapore's on crowded shelves, jar of all-day suckers on the counter, ice cream a dime.

Twenty blocks north, at 6th and Clark, Ken Lum's cross illuminates the neighbourhood night:

E
VAN
S
T

Godawful, say detractors. *Sticks it to The Man*, say those who applaud. Facebook the new graffiti wall. History. Competing still with pride.

Main Street

I grew up in an immigrant neighbourhood,
learned early *the banks and braes*, the pipes
skirling, Hogmanay and first footing, Culloden
and the Farquharson tartan: that was home—

The neighbours taught, too—not seamlessly—
adults drew lines around colour, their skin
prickled when German words showed up
in the bakery window—

But hand-me-downs rip and fade: we learned
chopsticks and garlic,
     gung haggis fat choy—

This is a praise poem:

for the public school,
     where cultures mix to become now,
     the lion dance as everyday as
     Robbie Burns and Hallowe'en—

for the idea of Vancouver neighbourhood,
     which no longer paints living space
     by colour, language, filiation—

for crossing meaningless lines, for talking over
     fences, for walkers' right-of-way, for
     public space to meet in, share—

We do not stop hearing the pipes and sitar,
cymbals, fiddles, dulcimer, drums—
But the past does not fix us: our children
sing their own songs, wear their own clothes—

If we choose, we will learn who we are
from the breath of our grandchildren:

Praise them—

Nick Names

1. lots of neighbourhoods had their moments, or what we call *their moments*, as though we missed something we think is more real than now:

2. *Robsonstrasse* before fashion claimed it: South Granville, when Szasz's cooked schnitzel: Theatre Row, when the traffic ran there, neon blazed, and Scott's was the only fancy restaurant in town:

3. or no—4th Avenue when the hippies had it tie-dyed and beaded, *yeah man* and *cool*, the whole world *waiting for the sunrise*—before Tom Terrific used the War Measures Act to round them up, postpone Aquarius: when the *Straight* began, and Greenpeace:

4. though always, before them, something else:

5. inside locale, you think you belong if you know the short forms—The Cut, The Drive, The Cultch—as though only one made sense, the real article:

6. those others—the ones trotted out as THE signs of *savoir faire*—Orpheum Stanley Capitol Strand—so many gone—though The Orpheum shows up opulent and arabesque just before the best scene in *The Imaginarium of Doctor Parnassus*—the claim's the same, just a different dream:

7. and *The Island, The Valley*? That's where you say you're from, where you go back to, all the rivalries

you've tried to leave behind, the ones you find
embarrassing but hold close, still need, the clumsy
bloody innocence of certainty:

8. on The Drive, you're already living together,
Mama's pasta out front, the olive oil *extra virgine*,
chourico Portuguese—arguing soccer over *caffe
nero* on the patio, and little theatres in back where
jazz is happening and even the future's possible—
but don't tell papa, not yet:

9. they cut a hole in the power grid, nick names—

Fortune Cookie

Dim sum on South Main with
seven friends, eights are good fortune:

the servers circle as though skating
figures, offer plates of music—

think gold mountain snowshine,
interplanetary spheres: the tumble and
ginger of green arpeggios, cymbal strike
and city horns—

each course dances, waits for us to choose,
or not choose,
to take part:

fluted trays of drumrolled spring,
garden partitas, suburb dumplings in
firework sauce:

the harmony, the flavour of this place:

good fortune: it is sweet
to be here—

Main Street

The thing is:

where King Edward crosses,
still,
the Windsor name shows up on signs:

I can't see it now without catching reruns,
the old Windsor Theatre,
long since levelled:

used to go there with a friend from school
who lived on the other side of Main:

we'd meet in front, pay our quarter, watch
Bogart films—lost treasure, Sam Spade—
or Gary Cooper in *Twelve O'clock High,*
far adventure just around the corner:

the thing is—   *the thing is,*
about losing touch,

years went by
before I heard he'd died:

by his own hand, whispered:

distance
                        every
time   un-
rolling un-
real:

Elegy

last night's rain hangs
   drop by
   drop on
   maple branches: black
        water buds

downpour darts upward
   sparking sharp off
   pavement—
   cuff and hem drench:
        cold fire

scotch mist gathers air
   in clusters,
   patches,
   brushes couriers
        in fern

showers scatter what we call
   here:
   a gnarl of dried sea grass,
   a mottled leopard's bane,
        pocked pool

Underpainting

Under overcast, umbrellas flower, burst like
    mushrooms out of folded shade, paint colour
    on the earth—pretense, pretense: the city thrives
    on what we do not see, the covert rainbows:

Versed in season, vagrant as weeds, they leap
    up from underground the moment rattle rains
    begin or nimbus hoods accumulate in packs
    or strips of sun flash promise, hoarfrost tease:

Reaching scarlet out of shrubbery, the dragon
    bowsprit of the *Empress of Japan* piercing the
    ocean's underbelly; across the harbour, red songs
    rising from shipyard workers, underemployed:

Outside a coffee shop, the scent of orange peel;
    in tiers at Granville Market, six rows of fledgling
    jack-o-lanterns; on dead cherry trees, bracket
    fungus; under logs, aleuria, amanita; rust:

Youth and ripeness on the opera stage, the star in
    ochre, regal, the understudy cadmium, caught
    in the footlights; sulfur piles on the foreshore, an
    underworld of pinnacles, mimic mountain peaks:

Greenpeace pamphlets, posted and underfoot, urging
    change, renewal, preservation; cedar fronds and moss
    bogs, jaded shepherds: grass-covered-winter's fir-
    scented air, the frayed grain of sap and shallow sea:

Beak tucked underwing, or *ready set* for downcast
    fish, a great blue heron motionless among the
    barnacles and periwinkled rocks, on display,
    one foot holding fast to secrets, underwater:

Ink-dark, indigo shadow on the rain-slicked street,
    signs on theatre row blinking as though under
    fire, neon stretching into river-run, reflection
    the inverse of the certain, a phantom undertow:

Vintage, like port and cellared wine, wild violets
    in fescue, wild rhododendrons stretching, sprawling
    purple into undergrowth: these colours dart and
    wheel beneath our grey disguise, underwriting light—

Dogwood

Salish speakers called it *Arrow-wood,*
Bow-wood—explaining how the bark,
roots, leaves could mix dye
or cure skins, adding
 The Cowichan use the word
 for knitting needles now—
   the sweaters, rain-resistant,
   wrapping us in eagles—

Naturalists use another speech,
write *cornus nuttalli,*
'horn' for the hardwood,
'Nuttall' for the British birdman, adding
 'dog, from *dag,* Sanskrit for skewers'—
   some dogged faith in Elsewhere
   swathing us in syllables—

Believers seek symbol,
 cruciform in the four-petal *cornus florida,*
   also called Blood-rag, Whiffle-tree,
   fall and rise again—

I ask only to see it live,
   shade-tolerant, Pacific
    it is in peril
   its six bracts drawing us
   twice this year, and twice every,
   into—say it—
     loveliness:
   into, under, in—

Moments

Stumbling into random beauty
   takes the breath away—
      gives us breath to live more:

so does the startle of contradiction—

   or do we startle contradiction into being
      (being as we are, contradictory:
         aspiring to more,
            immersed in the airless mundane)—

Beauty,
   random as red stones on a shelly beach,
      blue birds on a black branch
         after the second snowfall:
it waits to be seen—
         so feed on land's edge,
     salal ruffling the plain fabric of grass,
     arbutus bark peeling the rocks:

   the small things—

Places in this world stop us,
   hold us in contemplation:

some call them holy,

some simply shiver
   as though the dark rushes them
      on a hot day:

we are custodians of such places—
    call them *moments*:
they do not last,
    unless we notice them—

Water Garden

stone
stone
stone

each appearing
over the rushes

in the far pond at Van Dusen Gardens

to float

a child leaps forward, balancing

stoops
drops a pebble
watches rings embrace

a red carp flicks
disappears

a purple water lily

stone

Being

And some days
   stumbling into merriment—

a girl in yellow at Dunbar Park,
   pushing her little brother on a swing,
     laughter lifting like dandelion seed—

the wrinkled smile of the old mother
   resting in the moon-gate at Sun Yat-Sen,
     accordion lanterns hanging overhead,
       red as satisfaction—

somewhere
boys are scuffing a soccer ball
   round a dusty field, their voices
     pitched for dogs to hear, and
somewhere black labs and golden retrievers
perk up, stir, flump
   back on the floor
     in front of a heat register—

Merriment springs up,
               falls off,
folds the universe away,
   then spreads it out again
     in picnic and bells—

flare's not the key (paintbox of clowns,
        atomic puppetshow), just
something in the eye,
        connecting—

two rumpled men by the Terry Fox Monument
    exchanging recognition:
      even need feeds
          merriment, measuring
              one more day, lasting
                  one more day—

the privilege of being, when being happens,
and where—

Main Street

After a drift of suburb, I get to
33rd, abruptly aware (again) of
difference—off-Main changing along
with on—bicycle bells and Dickie Dee
still advertise a summer afternoon,
the bleachers at Nat Bailey cheer a
9th-inning run, hot dogs and mustard
prevail: but there's demolition where
social housing stood on Little Mountain's
eastern slope, *going, gone, over the fence
and out*, the scrubby crabgrass fields
uprooted for Development:

When we used to zigzag up that hill to the
reservoir (uncovered then and clear, now
underground), we always called it *Little
Mountain*, never *Queen Elizabeth Park*—

How much we live in the flux of words,
as though 400 feet was mountainous, as
though *Little* would curb an old volcano:
names   disappear—even *Lulu Island*'s
altered, *Miss Lulu Sweet* of San Francisco's
vanished into anecdote: *feng shui* replaces
her, the wind-water richness of *Richmond*—
(*dwelling*, from *duelian*, to go astray):

In my dreams of childhood, the sun
always shines: in dreams of childhood,
it always rains: it is the *always* that we
dream of, living every day in change:

At 49th, nearing my old neighbourhood,
is it myself I'm looking for? the grey false
fronts have gone, the ramshackle stores:
the *land agent* sports a chain realty marquee,
the *drug store*'s plus-sized: Punjabi
Market's open, dancing to *bhangra* rhythms,
feasting on *barfi*, seasoning the air with
coriander, *garam masala*: I am only
close to home ground:

Old duffers in baseball caps complain of
sandalwood and grass (who uses a word
like *duffer* any more?), but they mix with
the crowd: a college sprawls where I used to
practise what I once called *golfing*, on the
bush edge of a clipped Langara green:
what do I reinvent now, reaching here:
how do I change, having left to return:

I am caught up in rainbows, imagining
all of the city passing by: maybe I'll see
Vaisakhi celebrations, harvest chanting,
wheat-sheaf and orange turban: maybe Miss
PNE with a daffodil sash and glittering
tiara, one fuchsia-gloved hand waving
slow from a cobalt convertible: maybe
pipers in scarlet and jade, jazzing *Big
Yellow Taxi, The Grand Hotel, C'mon
and Roar You Lions Roar, Solidarity
Forever*:

I listen for the earth to move: a thousand
sari shops spill dazzle onto the sidewalk,
the flash of spring azaleas:

Brobdingnag

The grammar of giants
  is never the same
    as what you read in stories:

never
     Fee-fi-foe
     and a passel of thunderbolts,
not even
     Douglas firs and Banana slugs and
     lumbering massive nouns:
     mountain, tsunami, megafault, maze—

no:
    giants are ordinary here,
    the gigabytes of neighbourhood:
      they talk the grammar of doing,
      connecting,
      stepping out radical acts of simple gesture.

And you know them, the giants:
you call them
     Maud, Millie, Morrie, Mel,
you laugh together over the back fence, talk
     taxes and seedlings,
     traffic and the sound of children:

or you meet at a corner, pushing a trolley,

     I seen that thing yer lookin' for,
     I found this you c'n have it, Haven't

seen ya since last thursday,
        ya bin ok?
speech a pause in the process of living,
an affirmation of being, yes,
alive—

Unfolding

the paper shop on Powell
    reopens quietly,
    years after Evacuation—

the sign on the door says *Welcome,*
    each book a small butterfly,
    handcrafted—

bonsai and bamboo
    shape rock and water,
    branching landscapes—

       runic, paper folds
       open like gold sunrise:
       fall chrysanthemums —

Main Street

and then I'm tumbling suddenly steep
down the last long hill towards Marine: small
lots and dodgy clapboard sheds, Vancouver
Specials, California stucco:

the South Slope's *the best land in the city*,
my grandfather said, for growing:

roses and boys:

how do I find my way, pitching forward,
heading back: among warehouse mazes
where market gardens used to thrive:
sawdust mounds and sand, the new middens:

lines dissolve:

the current's still strong where Simon Fraser
once paddled towards the river's mouth: where
the Musqueam turned him back, resisting:

water swirling into the salt Strait,
eddying over the mudflats, sweeping
south, west, north around the Point, lapping the
freighters fast anchored in demurrage, edging
back to the Inlet The Captain named
for his friend Sir Harry Burrard,

where the Squamish live
and the Tsleil-waututh,
where Main Street begins all over again:

Alternatives

Cyclists
    step off the seabus,
        helmeted and keen,
            push their way into traffic,
                ride:

Follow them, watch them
    navigate the city, some with the flow,
        some like the unruly drivers they roundly
            condemn, cocking a snook as though
                drunk and in charge of courtesy:

Go with them, routine behind you—
    new space could be yours—step
        off Main, take Carrall, Keefer, onto paths
        that will lead you toward Seaside,
            Ridge, the Greenway:

In time take Balaclava, Windsor, off the grid—
    but learn first the narrow lane between
    concrete and poverty:
        the wheel turns as you ask it to—
            listen to its revolution:

Does it shout INSTEAD or celebrate AS WELL?
    leave in place the gates of discard,
        the boundary that mutters *me, not you*—
        or does it move beyond the lines,
            question OR itself,

look again
for the good land to grow in,
fresh creeks to run,

nothing less:

Bridge 3

Every year by the river's edge, standing
somewhere near the foot of Fraser, Main,

I remember the salmon run—sockeye, coho,
pink, Chinook, chum—the old Twigg Island

Bridge so low it used to swing wide for
every tug and boom—we used to joke

it would do the same if an extra large
herring asked to swim upstream—

    Tugboats still ply the river, haul
    logs to sawmills, barges out to sea:

    Trawlers still watchful, the long line
    to the hemlock boom, the stack of
    red containers,   snappable:
                no time for inattention:
      tugs nose-ready (workhorse powerhouse)

      the pull of the sea—

The bridge demolished now, and Ebisu
marooned: I dream of T-shirts blazoned

    RUN TO STOP EXTINCTION—

Home, away—   a site of absence
and tricks of memory—

Blue Boxes

City of cranes, long necks long legs stretching
steel into sky,

by day, noise, the whirr of life, the clank of
beam, buzzer, blue-collar rivet and weld:

>   *heaven within reach*:

On collection day, in the back lanes,
blue boxes fill with rubble and old
stories: the air stirs, and in the night
the cranes fly—

Old men who sit backwards
at the #3 bus stop downtown are watching
longevity: they're drawing
dots across the dark, outlining
beak and wings: scattering lotus, red
peony, awaiting flight:

When the ancient Celts who painted their faces blue
saw cranes fly overhead and erase the far horizon,
they said the world would appear to change
but not change:

>   a thousand white feathers
>   falling like deception:

Crabs

Off-leash at the dog parks (CRAB for one, where Main Sreet lets go of north and curls unexpectedly around to Portside), wire-haired terriers and desperate dachshunds twist and leap to catch yellow tennis balls in mid-air—you can almost hear them laughing—

CRAB—the acronym survives from protest placards: CREATE A REAL AVAILABLE BEACH: the park claims space along the water side of the railway tracks. Sunset here laps crane, dock, mussel-crusted stone—streams red across the skittering foreshore—the Salish name's *luk'luk'i*—

Rows of chained logs line other beaches—the sands of Kitsilano, the flats of English Bay, arranged marriages of tidiness and shell. Flotsam tumbles only onto *no beach*, onto barnacles below Pigott Park where shore crabs scramble maps of disarray—

In Coastal stories, Frog is sometimes called *Crab-of-the-Woods*: she's the shaman, speaks with the people's voice, carries messages between land and water, she understands the in-between:

I do not know if Salish star-gazers had a name for the faint constellation the ancient Greeks called Cancer, the Crab, or if they made its pincers a water sign of prophecy:

just that time and again we seek the intertide, to watch ourselves stand upright, scuttle out of the sea, catch our breath and laugh, believing we can fly—

Circle

Musqueam names still
whisper the landscape here,
     musqueam, the seagrass,
but is anyone listening?

I want to say *yes*,
but stumble over
     learning to—

no closer, even standing beneath
the Welcome arms that
Susan Point has carved at *Ulxen*'s tip:

hands offered,
readiness waiting for the honest request
     I ask permission to enter,
     I offer respect to the people,
     who are of the ocean, of the land.
     One with:

gesture transforms,
inscribes a circle:

Raven's aerial arc mirrors—
extends—Orca's submarine dive.

The Coast is human:
meeting place,
the present an always opportunity
to honour *nature, us,*
     being one—

Terminal

Go down to the river again, clamber
down among the saplings, step out

onto the sand: do you notice any foot-
prints? Greyweather houseboats used to dock

beside the booming-grounds: only a leaden
key-ring signs where a guy-rope once held

fast. Maybe you remember peaveys and pike-
poles flash in the morning sun, or timber-marks

on sawn ends of Douglas firs: or maybe
you imagine them, and birling games, and

salvage logs amassing at the shore. Look up,
away: YVR's on the other side, behind the dike,

bright with promises of Elsewhere, batteried
by rules, illusions, loud with scurry.

At the end of the runway, Sea Island
drifts into rivermouth: and words, like tugs,

bob off in the tide. Collector, castaway,
what do you tie your house to now?

The delta's afloat, mere particles of earth,
suspended for the moment, choosing to stay—

the rest, the river's running, saplings' reaching,
tell of distance, moving, closing in—

New Year

And after all I love this place, the scent of
spring, green leaf in the west wind, budding heat,
the sudden flick of March when down gives way
to tees and tease:

Spanish Banks, sand chasing the summer tide
halfway to China, castles in the air,
tree-forts and car-hops and playground pealing,
living the curve of the hours later,
tuned to the ocean: *skookum*:

bright snow on the Tantalus Range, the crisp
of mid-October just before leaf mountain,
the pile of topsoil promising renewal,
heritage crops at the farmers' market,
Trout Lake, Kitsilano, Riley Park, Mole Hill:

even winter's grey, the stipple on glass-
slick Granville, the burst of Christmas houselights,
Hogmanay and fiery Diwali,
Hannukah, Samhain, Nowruz, then Pender's
blazing cymbals, the dragon's year, the pig's,
the tiger's, beginning again, sweet
with a stem gift of oranges:

Main Street

yes—I live *here*, celebrate
the blackberry sweetness of uncertainty, raw
raven's voice, boggy waterland, green
seas of sedge and salal: and sing

> *here*, the wild still with us: *bears*
> *descend the mountains, berry-shy*
> *in search of food: coyotes cruise the inner*
> *city, shelties slack in their jaws*—

I sing *despite* as well as *here*, sing *because*, sing
>   *riptide moon, alley scrap, land's rim,* on
edge sing
yes—here is

difference, or would be:
the sawtooth Coast a river of traffic,
a shingle house of inter-
ruption:

> *bridgedeck,*
> *seafog,*
> *eagleshadow,*
> *undertow*—

Listen to the earth that tumbles beneath us:
its music, *yes*,

> shocks,
> erupts,
> settles,

sleeps,

is breathing
space,

as perfect, imperfect,
as rain:

ACKNOWLEDGMENTS

With thanks to Laurie Ricou and Ron Smith, who read early drafts and encouraged me to hear the rhythms of the city I remember as well as the sounds of the one I see; to Randal Macnair for his continuing commitment to poetry; and to other friends, nearby and online, who with remarkable restraint over three long years listened to me talking about *then and now.*

With love to Peggy and to my extended family, who every day remind me of history's presence and the living room of home.

And with appreciation, for his laughter, his words, and his years of thoughtfulness, to Robert Kroetsch.

Born and raised in Vancouver, W.H. New has travelled widely, and in books of both poetry and prose he has written extensively about the social and personal importance of place. In *Borderlands* he asks how Canadians talk about Canada, and in works such as *Touching Ecuador* and *Grandchild of Empire* he draws on his encounters with societies abroad. His many other publications include *Underwood Log* (shortlisted for the Governor General's Award for Poetry), the *Encyclopedia of Literature in Canada*, and *Vanilla Gorilla* (one of several books for children).

His writing has received international recognition, including the Lorne Pierce Medal, the Governor General's International Award in Canadian Studies, and the Lion & Unicorn Honour Book Award for North American poetry for children (for *The Year I Was Grounded*). He was appointed an Officer of the Order of Canada in 2006.

In *YVR*, his tenth book of poetry, William New turns his attention back to his home city.